Celebrate the Savior's Birth

ISBN 0-7935-8454-X

HAL•LEONARD®
CORPORATION
7777 W. BLUEMOUND RD. P.O. BOX 13819 MILWAUKEE, WI 53213

Visit Hal Leonard Online at
www.halleonard.com

ANGELS FROM THE REALMS OF GLORY

Words by JAMES MONTGOMERY
Music by HENRY SMART

Joyfully

An - gels from the realms of glo - ry,

Wing your flight o'er all the earth,

Ye who sang cre - a - tion's sto - ry,

Now pro - claim Mes - si - ah's birth.

G7 — Come and wor - ship! | C — F — Come and wor - ship!

Dm — F — Wor - ship Christ the | G7 — C — new - born King!

C — Sa - ges, leave your | con - tem - pla - tions,

F — C/E — Bright - er vis - ions | G7/D — C — beam a - far,

E
Seek the great De - sire of na - tions
Am G/D D7 G
Ye have seen His na - tal star.
G7 C F
Come and wor - ship! Come and wor - ship!
Dm F G7 C
Wor - ship Christ the new - born King!

AWAY IN A MANGER

Anonymous Text (vv.1,2)
Text by JOHN T. McFARLAND (v.3)
Music by JONATHAN E. SPILLMAN

Slow Waltz

A - way in a __ man - ger no crib for a

bed, The lit - tle Lord Je - sus lay down His sweet

head. The stars in the ___ heav - en looked

down where he lay. The lit - tle Lord Je - sus a -

sleep on the hay. The ___ cat - tle are low - ing, the

poor ba - by wakes; But ___ lit - tle Lord Je - sus no

cry - ing____ he____ makes. I love thee Lord____

Je - sus look down from the sky And

stay by my cra - dle to watch lul - la - by.

THE BIRTHDAY OF A KING

Anonymous Text
Music by WILLIAM H. NEIDLINGER

Tenderly

In a / lit – tle vil – lage of / Beth – le – hem there
hum – ble birth – place, but / Oh! how much there God

lay a Child one / day, / and the
gave to us one that / day, / from the

sky was bright with a / ho – ly light, o'er the
man – ger bed, what a / path has led, what a

place where Je – sus / lay. / Al – le –
per – fect ho – ly way. /

C7 ... **F** ...

lu - ia _____ oh, how the an - gels sang, al - le -

G7 **C**

lu - ia _____ oh, how the cho - rus rang. And ___ the

F **Bb** **F** **C7** **F** **Bb**

sky was bright with a ho - ly light, 'twas the

F/C **C7** **F** **F**

1. **2.**

birth - day of a King. 'Twas a King.

COME, THOU LONG EXPECTED JESUS

Words by CHARLES WESLEY
Music by ROWLAND HUGH PRICHARD

Come,
Born,
Thou
Thy
long _____ ex -
peo - ple

pect - ed
to de -
Je - sus,
liv - er,
Born to
Born a

D Gm C7 F
set Thy peo - ple free. From our
child and yet a king. Born to
Gm C7
fears and sins re - lease us;
reign in us for - ev - er,
Am C♯dim7 D C7
Let us find our rest in
Now Thy gra - cious king - dom
F F/C Gm/C
Thee. Is - rael's strength and con - so -
bring. By Thine own e - ter - nal

C7
la - tion, Hope of all the earth Thou
Spir - it Rule in all our hearts a -
C Am C7 F
art; Dear de - sire of ev - 'ry
lone. By Thine all - suf - fi - cient
C7 D7 Gm
na - tion, Joy of ev - 'ry
mer - it Raise us to Thy
F/C C7 1. F 2. F
long - ing heart.
glo - rious throne.

THE FIRST NOEL

17th Century English Carol

Majestically

mf

The —

C — first — No - el — **G/B** up — the — **F** an - gel **G** did **F**

look - ed — and — saw — a

C say, **G7** was to **Am** cer - tain **Em** poor **F** shep - herds **C** in **D7** **G7**

star shin - ing in — the east — be -

C fields as **G7** they **C** lay, **G** In — **C** fields — where **G/B** they lay —

yond — them far, And — to — the — earth it —

F G F C G7 Am Em F C D7 G7
keep - ing their sheep on a cold win - ter's night that
gave great light and so it con - tin - ued both
C G7 C G C Em
was so deep. No - el, No - el, No -
day and night.
F C Am G F C F G
el, No - el, Born is the King of
1. C G7 C G
2. C G7 C
Is - ra - el. They
Is - ra - el.
rall.

THE FRIENDLY BEASTS

Traditional English Carol

Gently

Lyrics:

Je - sus, our broth - er kind and good, Was
And ev' - ry beast by some and good spell In the

hum - bly born in a sta - ble rude. And the
sta - ble dark was glad to tell Of the

friend - ly beasts a - round Him stood,
gift - ly He gave Em - man - u - el,

Je - sus, our broth - er kind and good.
The gift He gave Em - man - u - el.

O COME, ALL YE FAITHFUL
(Adeste Fidelis)

Words and Music by JOHN FRANCIS WADE
Latin Words translated by FREDERICK OAKELEY

Moderately
G D
f
O come, all ye faith - ful,
G D G Am G D Em D A
Joy - ful and tri - um - phant, O come ye, O
D G D A7 D
come ye to Beth - le - hem;
G D7 G D G D Em Am D G
Come and be - hold Him, born the King of an - gels; O

come, let us a - dore Him, O come, let us a - dore him, O come, let us a - dore him, __ Christ __ the Lord.

Sing choirs of an - gels, sing in ex - ul - ta - tion, O sing all ye ci - ti - zens of heav - en a -

bove.

Glo - ry to God _____

in ___ the ___ high - est O come, let us a -

dore Him, O come, let us a - dore Him, O come, let us a

dore Him, _____ Christ, _____ the Lord!

GO TELL IT ON THE MOUNTAIN

African-American Spiritual

Moderately

Go, tell it on the moun - tain

O - ver the hills and ev - ery - where, Go, tell it on the

moun - tain that Je - sus Christ _ is born. The

shep - herds feared and trem - bled When lo! a - bove the

G/D Bm Em A7
earth Rang out the an - gel cho - rus That hailed our Sav - ior's
D7 G Am G Am G Am
birth Go, tell it on the moun - tain, o - ver the hills and
G Am G Am G
Ev - ery - where, Go, tell it on the moun - tain that
Am D7 G
Je - sus Christ is born.
rit.

GOD REST YE MERRY, GENTLEMEN

19th Century English Carol

Spirited

God rest ye mer - ry gen - tle - men, let

noth - ing you dis - may   For Je - sus Christ our

B♭ A
Sav - ior was born on Christ - mas day To
Gm C F Gm F A Dm C F C7 Dm C
save us all from Sa - tan's power when we were gone a - stray. O
F B♭ F Dm A7 Dm C
ti - dings of com - fort and joy, com-fort and joy. O
F Dm A7 Dm
ti - dings of com - fort and joy.

GOOD CHRISTIAN MEN, REJOICE

14th Century German Melody

Moderately

mf Good Christ - tian men, re - joice _____ with
Christ - tian men, re - joice _____ with

heart and soul and voice, _____
heart and soul and voice, _____

Give ye heed to what we say:
Now ye hear of end - less bliss;

News! News! Je - sus Christ is
Joy! Joy! Je - sus Christ was

Dm

born to - day!
born for this.

F

Ox and ass be -
He hath ope'd the

Dm

fore Him bow, And
heav'n - ly door, And

Gm7 **C7**

He is in the
man is bless - ed

Dm

man - ger now;
ev - er - more.

B♭ **C7**

Christ is born to -
Christ was born for

F **Am**

day! _____
this! _____

F/C **C7**

Christ is born to -
Christ was born for

1. **F**

day. _____ Good

2. **F**

this! _____

HARK! THE HERALD ANGELS SING

Words by CHARLES WESLEY
Music by FELIX MENDELSSOHN-BARTHOLDY

Moderately

G D G D
Joy - ful all ye na - tions rise
G D G D
Join the tri - umph of the skies;
C E7 Am E Am
With th' an - gel - ic host pro - claim,
D G D G
"Christ is born in Beth - le - hem."

Hark! The her - ald an - gels sing, "Glo - ry ____ to the

new - born King!"

Fine

Sing we all of the Sa - vior mild.

Through long a - ges ____ of the past,
O how lov - 'ly ____ O how pure

Proph - ets have be -
Is this per - fect ____

told His com - ing,
Child of heav - en

Through long a - ges ____ of the past;
O how lov - 'ly ____ O how pure,

1.
Am   G   D7

Now the time has ____ come at last!
Gra - cious gift of ____

2.
Am   G   D7
D.S. al Fine

God to man!

IN THE BLEAK MIDWINTER

Poem by CHRISTINA ROSSETTI
Music by GUSTAV HOLST

Lyrics (line 1):
1. In the bleak mid-
2. God, heav'n can-not
3.-5. *See additional lyrics*

win - ter
hold him,

frost - y wind made
nor _____ earth sus -

moan,
tain.

earth stood hard as
Heav'n and earth as shall

i - ron,
flee away

wa - ter like a
when He like comes to

stone.
reign.

Snow had fall - en
In the fall bleak mid -

snow on snow,
win - ter

Additional Lyrics

3. Enough for Him, whom cherubim
   Worship night and day,
   A breastful of milk
   And a mangerful of hay.
   Enough for Him, whom angels
   Fall down before,
   The ox and ass and camel
   Which adore.

4. Angels and archangels
   May have gathered there,
   Cherubim and seraphim
   Thronged the air.
   But only his mother
   In her maiden bliss
   Worshipped the Beloved
   With a kiss.

5. What can I give Him,
   Poor as I am?
   If I were a shepherd,
   I would give a lamb.
   If I were a wise man,
   I would do my part.
   Yet what can I give Him,
   Give Him my heart.

INFANT HOLY, INFANT LOWLY

Traditional Polish Carol

Sweetly
G D7 Em
mp
D7 G D
p mp
In - fant ho - ly, in - fant low - ly, for his
sleep - ing, shep - herds keep - ing vig - il
G C D7 G
bed a cat - tle stall; ox - en low - ing, lit - tle
till the morn - ing new saw the glo - ry, heard the

know - ing, Christ the babe is Lord of all. Swift are
sto - ry, tid - ings of a gos - pel true. Thus re -

wing - ing an - gels sing - ing, no - els ring - ing, tid - ings
joic - ing, free from sor - row, prais - es voic - ing, greet the

bring - ing: Christ the Babe is Lord of all.
mor - row: Christ the Babe was born for you.

Flocks were you.

IT CAME UPON THE MIDNIGHT CLEAR

Words by EDMUND H. SEARS
Music by RICHARD STORRS WILLIS

Gently

It came up - on the mid - night clear, that glo - ri - ous song of old, From an - gels bend - ing near the earth to touch their harps of gold. Peace

E7 Am E Am
on the earth; Good will to men from
G D7 G
heav - en's all gra - cious King. The
p
C F C F C
world in sol - emn still - ness lay to
F G7 C
hear the an - gels sing.

JOY TO THE WORLD

Words by ISAAC WATTS
Music by GEORGE F. HANDEL

Moderately

G/B
sing, And heaven and na - ture sing, And
love, And won - ders of His love, And
Am F C Dm C/G G
heav - en and heav - en and na - ture
won - ders, won - ders of His
1. C
sing.
2. C
love.
F
G7
C

MARY HAD A BABY

African-American Spiritual

Slowly, with expression

Pedal optional

Mary had a ba-by, my Lord.
Laid him in a man-ger, my Lord,
Mary had a ba-by, laid him in a man-ger,

my Lord.
my Lord.
Mary had a ba-by,
Mary had a ba-by,
Mary had a ba-by, laid him in a man-ger,

1.
2.
D7
Dm7♭5
C
Dm7♭5
C
Ma - ry had a ba - by,
my Lord.
What did she call him,
Ma - ry had a ba - by,
my Lord.
She called him Je - sus,
F
C
Em
Gsus
G
my Lord?
What did she call him,
my Lord?
my Lord.
She called him Je - sus,
my Lord.
Am
C/G
Fmaj7
Am
D7
Ma - ry had a ba - by,
what did she call him,
Ma - ry had a ba - by,
Ma - ry had a ba - by,
she called him Je - sus,
Ma - ry had a ba - by,
1.
2.
R.H. 8va
Fm
C
Fm
C
D7
Fm
C
my Lord.
my Lord.
p
rit.

O COME, O COME IMMANUEL

Traditional Melody
Words translated by JOHN M. NEALE
and HENRY S. COFFIN

Freely
Em
Am
Bm
Em
mf
O
Em
Am
Em
come, O come Im - man - u - el, and
Am
Bm
Em
ran - som cap - tive Is - ra - el, that
Am
Em
D
Em
mourns in lone - ly ex - ile here un - til the Son of

God _____ ap - pear. Re - joice, re - joice! Im -

man - u - el shall come to Thee, O

Is - ra - el! O come, Thou key of Da - vid,

come and o - pen wide our heav'n - ly home. Make

safe the way that leads _____ on high and close the path to

mis - er - y. Re - joice, re - joice! Im -

man - u - el shall come to Thee, O Is - ra -

el!

Ped. *

O HOLY NIGHT

French Words by PLACIDE CAPPEAU
English Words by D.S. DWIGHT
Music by ADOLPHE ADAM

Slow and Solemn (in 2, ♩ = 1 beat)

O ho - ly night,____ the stars are bright - ly

shin - ing; It is the night of the dear Sav - ior's

birth.____ Long lay the world____ in

sin and er - ror pin - ing, Till He ap - peared and the

soul felt its worth. _____ A thrill of

hope, the wear - y soul re - joic - es, For yon - der

breaks a new and glo - rious morn. Fall _____

_____ on your knees, _____ Oh hear _____

the an - gel voic - es! O night di - vine, _____ O night _____ when Christ was born! O night, O ho - ly night, O night di - vine!

O LITTLE TOWN OF BETHLEHEM

Words by PHILLIPS BROOKS
Music by LEWIS H. REDNER

OF THE FATHER'S LOVE BEGOTTEN

13th Century Plainsong

Reverently

1. Of the Fa - ther's love be - got - ten,
2.-4. *(See additional lyrics)*

ere the worlds be - gan _____ to be,

He is Al - pha and O - me - ga,

He the Source, the End - ing He.

Of the things that are, that have _____ been,

And that fu - ture years shall see,

Ev - er - more and ev - er - more! _____

Additional Lyrics

2. O that birth forever blessed,
    When the Virgin, full of grace,
    By the Holy Ghost conceiving
    Bare the Savior of our race;
    And the Babe, the world's Redeemer,
    First revealed His sacred face,
    Evermore and evermore!

3. O ye heights of heav'n, adore Him;
    Angel hosts, His praises sing.
    Pow'rs, dominions, bow before Him,
    And extol our God and King.
    Let no tongue on earth be silent,
    Ev'ry voice in concert ring,
    Evermore and evermore!

4. Christ, to Thee with God the Father,
    And, O Holy Ghost, to Thee,
    Hymn and chant and high thanksgiving
    And unwearied praises be;
    Honor, glory, and dominion,
    And eternal victory,
    Evermore and evermore!

SILENT NIGHT

Words by JOSEPH MOHR
Music by FRANZ GRUBER

Slowly

Si - lent night, night, Ho - ly
Si - lent night, night, Ho - ly

with pedal

night! All is calm,
night! Shep - herds quake

all is bright. Round yon
at the sight. Glo - ries

Vir - gin Moth - er and Child
stream from heav - en a - far,

C ... **G7** ... **C**

rests in ___ slum - ber | while we ___ pray in | end - less ___ num - ber.
heav - en ___ sing - ing | songs of ___ ju - bi - | la - tion ___ bring - ing.

C/B ... **Am** ... **C/G** ... **Dm/F** ... **G7**

Still, ___ still, ___ | still, ___ to ___ | sleep is ___ now His ___
Sleep, ___ sleep, ___ | sleep, while ___ | we Thy ___ vi - gil ___

1
2

1. **C** ... **2.** **C** ... *Both hands 8va - - - - - - - - - - - - - - - - -* ... **C/B**

will. | keep. | Sleep, ___ sleep, ___

Am ... **C/G** ... **Dm/F** ... **G7** ... **C**

sleep, | while ___ we Thy ___ vi - gil ___ | keep.

rit.

1
2

3

SWEET LITTLE JESUS BOY

African-American Spiritual

Sweetly, tenderly

Sweet lit - tle Je - sus boy, they made you be born in a man - ger. Sweet lit - tle ho - ly child; and we did - n't know who you were. Did - n't know you'd come to save us, Lord, to take our sins a - way. Our

eyes were blind, we could not

see, _____ and we did - n't know who you were.

You have ___ shown us now, we are ___

try - in'. _____

C

Mas - ter, you have ___ shown us how

Am Em Am

e - ven when you were dy - in'. ___

F G C

Just seems like we

G C Em

can't do right.

F G Am

Look how we treat - ed you.

G C Em

But

F G

please, _____

Am

Sir, for - give us,

Em F

Lord. _____ We did – n't know it was you.

Sweet lit – tle Je – sus boy, born long time a –

go. _____ Sweet _____ lit – tle Ho – ly Child, and we

did – n't know who you were.

WE THREE KINGS OF ORIENT ARE

Words and Music by
JOHN H. HOPKINS

Gently and quietly

We three Kings of O - ri - ent are;

Bear - ing gifts we tra - verse a - far,

Field and foun - tain, moor and moun - tain,

fol - low - ing yon - der star. O_____

*Implied harmony

star of won - der, star of night,

Star with roy - al beau - ty bright,

West - ward lead - ing, still pro - ceed - ing,

guide us to thy per - fect light.

WHAT CHILD IS THIS?

Words by WILLIAM C. DIX
16th Century English Melody

Gently, not too slow

What child is this who laid to rest on
Mar - y's lap is sleep - ing? Whom
an - gels greet with an - thems sweet while
shep - herds watch are keep - ing.

This, this is Christ the King, whom
shep - herds guard and an - gels sing.
Haste, haste to bring Him laud the
babe the son of Mar - y.

WHILE SHEPHERDS WATCHED THEIR FLOCKS

Words by NAHUM TATE
Music by GEORGE F. HANDEL

Moderately

While __ shep - herds watched their

flocks by __ night, All __ seat - ed on the __ ground, __ The __

an - gel of the Lord came __ down, and __ glo - ry shone a -

round, _____ And glo - ry shone a - round.